How to write an email
How to be a boss
How to cry at work
How to quit your job

extracurricularpress.com

Agenda

Agenda

Introduction

I've been planning my corporate survival guide series for the past five years and it was always intended to support people through the full arc of a career, from the learning stages (*How to write an email*) through the mess of middle management (*How to be a boss*) and then finally on to exit plans and new adventures (*How to quit your job*).

But something unexpected happened on the way to completing my workplace trilogy. I found myself at a new job with new people, surrounded by a culture where crying and complaining were commonplace. I realized that my foolproof system of communication and operational excellence had failed to address an entire overture of the work-a-day experience, namely, the emotions of work.

This book is not just about crying—although it will help you understand why people might cry in the workplace and how to react appropriately. This book is a guide to navigating the emotions of working with other human beings as well as the surprising number of emotions involved with filling out spreadsheets, sending emails, giving presentations and missing deadlines.

Any time human beings are involved in anything, it is going to be emotional. Especially when you confine a semi-random group of people to a building and ask them to do the same thing over and over and over again for an extended period of time, the recipe is combustible. When we add the fact that everyone is coming into work from different backgrounds and often for completely different reasons the potential for intense emotions and outright confusion is not only probable, it's guaranteed.

It would be easy to indulge in a laundry list of why it's so hard to work with other people. It would be tempting to commiserate about the complexity of the human condition and it's countless corresponding emotions, but I prefer to do the more difficult thing and explain why it doesn't need to be that complicated. Nuanced, yes—complicated and overwhelming, no.

As I pointed out at the beginning of my book, *How to be great at your job*, people have a tendency (or perhaps it's an unconscious desire) to get wrapped up in the perceived injustices of workplace politics, interpersonal drama, bad bosses, competing priorities or unrealistic deadlines. But the reality is much simpler than that. If you just do a few basic things right, traversing the landscape of work can be easy—and fun.

That said, it's important to acknowledge the pervasive hierarchies of privilege—structural, racial, gendered—that persist in the workplace no matter where you live and work. Life isn't fair, and neither is work—so part of my job is to shine a light on where we fall short and how it impacts everyone we work with.

A lot of what you'll read in this book could be dismissed as common sense, but sometimes there is power in seeing something written down and stripped of all its pomp and circumstance.

In this book, we will confront many assumptions about the

emotions of work and lay them bare. We will investigate how to move your approach from one of passive victim ("I have a bad boss", "This person doesn't like me") into one of radical personal responsibility.

We will explore how the foundation to a healthy emotional performance at work is understanding your own emotional triggers so you can restructure your communications, your schedule and your reactions in such a way to mitigate the downside. We will also look at how stress can quickly escalate from low-level anxiety ("There's a lot going on") to thinking too much to you sucking at your job. We will examine the impact you have on the people around you through the lens of nine behaviors to start practicing and three things to never do again. We will talk about crying at work, but we will also talk about emotional resilience and how to bring a bit of happiness into your work life.

Let's get to work.

1. Emoti
perfor

nal
nance

1. Emotional performance

This book is about managing the emotions of the workplace. But before we start talking about how to navigate your way through the minefields of working with other human beings, we need to replace the commonly used phrase *emotional intelligence* (something you have) with the more relevant descriptor *emotional performance* (something you do).

Whether you realize it or not, being good at your job is a performance. It is something you must do day in and day out for weeks and months and years on end from email to email, meeting to meeting and deadline to deadline with a rotating cast of characters and no time for rehearsals. It's a difficult act to keep up so it's a good idea to have a system by which you hold yourself together, keep yourself motivated and constantly prepare yourself for the next scene.

Our work day can be thought of as a series of overlapping performances along three fronts: operational (writing emails, organizing files, doing work), interpersonal (presentations, lunch, meetings) and emotional (disappointment, empathy, crying, stressing). And while the first two can be planned for, systematized and controlled to a large degree (Hint: read my books *How to write an email* and *How to be a boss*), it is the third—emotional performance—that is often the most difficult for people to understand and navigate effectively.

Managing your emotions isn't an all or nothing experience. It exists on a spectrum and it's important to acknowledge you (and the people around you) will have good moments and bad, doing the right thing at the right time in one situation and grossly misreading the impact of your words the next. It's life. It's human. It's messy.

Improving your emotional performance takes practice, readiness to embrace progress over perfection and, perhaps most important of all, willingness to forgive yourself—and others—when the reality falls short of your expectations.

The depths and meaning of emotions and outbursts in the workplace are unknowable in the extreme. Therefore I recommend an approach that takes into account your own personal emotional baggage, the people around you, and the pre-existing norms that color our collective experience of emotional performance from meeting to meeting, email to email, deadline to deadline.

- Past is prologue
- Know yourself
- Be aware of others
- Politics of emotion

Past is prologue

Shakespeare's famous phrase from *The Tempest*, "What's past is prologue," stands for the idea that previous experiences predict current behaviors, something that is too often overlooked in the emotional landscape of our day-to-day interactions with co-workers.

People don't cry because they missed a deadline, people cry because missing the deadline evokes an experience from their past. Maybe their dad punished them when they didn't meet expectations. Maybe they failed at another job in a similar way and are terrified to go through it all over again.

People don't yell at coworkers to test whether it is an effective management technique, people yell at coworkers because it's a learned behavior—something they observed from a young age when a parent, coach or sibling used a raised voice to get what they want.

Understanding that we all bring a world of experience and emotional baggage with us each day when we walk into our offices is an important first step in acknowledging that the emotions that come out from meeting to meeting are more often than not rooted in past experiences that transcend the specific moment we might find ourselves in with our co-workers.

In fact, we don't need to look into our distant childhood to find useful context for our co-worker's behavior at work. What's their home life like? Are they in a relationship? What financial responsibilities do they carry for their family? How is their health? Who was their former manager? What behaviors were rewarded or frowned upon at their last job? All of these experiences, distant and relatively recent will inform how you or your co-worker behaves or reacts in the workplace.

Know yourself

Before you try to solve other people's issues it's a good idea to be aware of your own. Nobody is perfect, so it is useful to admit to yourself that you have good days and bad days. You get frustrated, you get overtired, you get grouchy or hangry or disappointed too.

It's not easy to be self-aware. That's why most people just blame their boss for everything that goes wrong. But when considering your own emotional performance at work it's useful not only to acknowledge the outcomes that are highly visible (raising your voice, crying, shutting down, cutting someone off) but also to investigate the underlying triggers that cause these behaviors.

Do you know what your emotional triggers are?

My trigger is time. I'm obsessed with getting things done on time—which to me means early. But in my efforts to deliver all of my work (and start my meetings) on time, I started acting out—speaking loudly and shutting people down. Everyone around me interpreted this as me being a jerk but the truth (which I was not aware of at the time) was that I was acting out emotionally because my co-workers were literally getting in the way of the thing that was most important to me: being on time.

Why was I reacting the way I was when someone was ten seconds late to a meeting? Why was I impatient when someone was taking too long to explain something to me? Why did I tend to cut people off towards the end of meetings?

It wasn't until I stopped to consider my own faults and inclinations that I was able to develop some semblance of self-awareness, which was the first—required—step towards actual empathy and a more effective emotional performance with my co-workers.

It took me five years to identify my triggers, but once I did, everything changed for the better. Meetings got easier, my team worked harder, my promotions happened faster and navigating the working world felt less stressful. I was finally able to avoid self-inflicted wounds that come with being unaware of your own emotional stress points.

So if you find yourself having to deal with a lot of "emotional" people at work I encourage you to take a step back and consider your own contribution to the situation first. Understand how you might be feeding into the emotional ecosystem and adjust your behavior accordingly.

It's not enough to "deal with" each emotional moment at work as it happens because you will soon be exhausted, frustrated and bogged down in the countless emotional traps that lurk within every human interaction. It is incumbent upon you to avoid as many of these moments as possible by first being aware of your own emotional triggers.

Be aware of others

How well do you know your co-workers? How much time do you spend with them outside of high-pressure, deadline-is-coming situations?

At work it's easy to fall into the trap of treating people differently depending on their titles, job descriptions or where they went to college. But these work filters get in the way of being able to recognize our co-workers as human beings, i.e. people with aunts, uncles, brothers, sick kids at home and a student loan payment due next week.

Acknowledging that we each have lives outside of work that inform how we behave and show up on a daily basis is a critical step towards navigating the emotions that come with each of us as individuals.

Knowing the people around you is also a form of self preservation. Some people are insecure, unreliable and prone to act out so it's a good idea to know who tends toward these extremes and adjust your interactions accordingly.

On the flip side, the better people know you, the more likely they are to understand your ups and downs and adjust their own behaviors to match the moment. Being able to give each other the benefit of the doubt when things go sideways or you have an awkward interaction is a win/win situation for everyone involved.

The other part of being aware of the people around you is knowing what makes someone tick. Understanding that what motivates one person may de-motivate another will inform (and change) how you interact with the people around you, better preparing you to meet the challenges of working within a team.

Getting to know the people around you doesn't have to be complicated or difficult. In fact, the more basic you keep it, the better, so start by learning everyone's name, saying good morning everyday and inviting different people to lunch or coffee to create room for conversations that extend beyond the next work deadline.

Re-orienting your approach to see your co-workers as human beings first and co-workers second will fundamentally alter your experience of working with other human beings. In a good way.

Politics of emotion

Knowing yourself and the people around you is critically important to being able to perform effectively at work everyday, but we cannot talk about emotional performance without acknowledging the unspoken assumptions, rules and inherited norms that provide the backdrop to how you and your co-workers treat each other, react to each other and judge each other.

How is it that a straight man can yell and he will be called a leader while a female co-worker who raises her voice will be labeled a bitch? Why is it that when women or gay men cry at work, people dismiss their emotions as weaknesses tied to their gender or sexual orientation? Why is it that someone's race or ethnicity affects perceptions of their performance? Is that fair? No. Is that the stereotype? Yes.

Lurking in all of our interactions is a generational and hierarchical skew that is informed by social privileges which have perpetuated the rights and norms of certain groups over others, leaving little or no room for different cultural backgrounds or traditions when it comes to the perceived "right way" to react or express oneself at work.

It's only recently (in the past five to ten years) that the conversation about privilege has come out in the open. We are at the very early stages of understanding (and unraveling) how centuries of bias inform every aspect of our work culture from the way we hire people to the way we celebrate holidays. Race, gender, education and sexual orientation inform every aspect of our experience as human beings, and while the fight for equality has been underway for some time, the journey to understanding and empathy is in its infancy.

Knowledge is power so it's important that you understand the prevailing stereotypes and perceptions that get attached to people that cry or yell at work as well as the systemic structural barriers that perpetuate advantages and disadvantages for yourself and your co-workers on a daily basis. It's easy to say these are wrong, and we will talk about how to correct them, but first let's acknowledge them so we all start on the same page.

2. Situat
aware

onal

ness

2. Situational Awareness

It is smart to be cognizant of the recurring situations where emotions tend to reveal themselves and have a plan for how to manage through (or around) them, setting yourself up for success while effectively side-stepping any potential downsides or emotional quagmires.

If you knew there was a speed trap on a certain road you'd adjust your behavior accordingly (slowing down or going around). It's much the same with work. If you know there are certain interactions that tend to lead to emotional confrontations it is only common sense to adjust your approach accordingly.

There is little upside to charged emotional interactions at work so it behooves everyone involved to have situational awareness and behave in ways (big and small) that decrease the likelihood of causing conflict. You can't avoid these moments, but you can be prepared for them.

We will spend the rest of the chapter going through the six most common situations in the workplace where potentially emotional interactions await you and your co-workers.

- Face to face conversations
- You screwed up
- Surprises
- Deadlines
- Group meetings
- Midyear + end of year reviews

Face to face conversations

Human interactions can be messy. Some people don't know how to explain what they want, some people are in too much of a rush and some people just suck at talking to other people.

Even the most basic conversations have the potential to be misinterpreted or misremembered. That's why writing things down and sending them in email quickly after any face to face discussions is the surest means of ensuring alignment and speeding the process of getting work done.

In my experience, getting things in writing can help to mitigate any future emotional turmoil of misunderstandings, frustrations or he said/she said confrontations. By recapping conversations, instructions, deadlines and expectations via quick, bullet-pointed email recaps, you are helping to keep everyone organized while at the same time giving yourself and your co-workers a non-emotional arbiter to whatever confusion might arise in the future.

It may feel like extra work to get things in writing but if a quick, thirty second email could help you avoid an awkward interaction with a co-worker—isn't that worth it?

Writing things down has the added benefit of allowing you time to organize your thoughts and feelings more clearly, usefully separating the facts from your feelings and in so doing, allowing you to better strike at the central truth of the situation. It can also give you a chance to more clearly make your case. A clean, crispy email with two to three bullet points can become your ambassador up the food chain, rather than relying on the voice-over from your manager or co-worker which can often result in an unfavorable game of telephone.

You screwed up

Mistakes happen. Deadlines get missed. Presentations don't go as planned. Important information gets overlooked. The list of what could go wrong on any given day is endless and should be accepted as a regular part of doing business. Therefore, it's best to have a strategy on how to react when things don't go as planned.

Contrary to popular instinct, when you find yourself at the center of such an instance, the cleanest, easiest and quickest way to move through a potentially emotional moment is to take responsibility: jump on the grenade.

The key to doing this effectively is to take SO MUCH responsibility that there is no further blame, emotion or anger that can exist around the issue. In essence, you are suffocating the situation by hugging it so tightly that it can't breathe—there is no oxygen with which to fan the flames—and in so doing, you effectively put out the fire before it even starts.

This can be accomplished by owning your mistake with simple sentences such as: "I made a mistake", "I screwed up", "This was my fault." The key is to keep it short and simple and never reach for excuses or add a "but" to the statement.

Put together, a good go-to phrase can be: "This was my fault. I'm sorry"—usually followed by a simple statement or question about how you will/should proceed from there.

When things go wrong, people instinctively look for someone to blame so by taking responsibility quickly at the start you allow people to move on to solving the problem rather than dwell in recriminations and finger pointing.

Another useful analogy to remember in moments such as these would be the infamous truism: The cover up is often worse than the crime. So when someone points out something that went wrong, simply reply "You're right..." and voila, a potentially emotional situation is immediately diffused and everyone moves on to the next issue and the next and the next and the next.

Surprises

Surprises are the enemy. Nobody likes surprises in the workplace. Bosses hate surprises. Co-workers hate surprises. Teams hate surprises. CFOs hate surprises. And before you even ask, there are no exceptions made for "good" surprises—unless you're throwing someone a party.

The word surprise comes from the Latin word for "seize" and originally referenced an unexpected military attack. When viewed through the context of emotions in the workplace, it's easy to understand that when people are surprised they have a tendency to react defensively and their emotions can often cloud an otherwise straightforward decision, request or negotiation.

Some simple actions you can take to avoid surprises and thus preempt any unnecessary emotional situations would be: Send agendas 24 hours in advance, send reminders about deadlines, repeat yourself early and often when it comes to priorities, give advance warning if you'll miss a deadline, and spend extra time to super clarify expectations before starting projects.

Deadlines

Deadlines are one of the few definitive moments of yes-or-no judgement in the workplace.

Either you hit the deadline or you miss it. For some this is a welcome chance to meet a clear expectation; for others, it's a high stakes emotional adventure filled with pressure and anxiety. Deadlines are an experience that can make both managers and co-workers act in ways and say things they might not otherwise recognize.

My prescription for managing the emotions around deadlines is simple: Don't miss deadlines.

Quite simply, there really is no excuse for missing deadlines at work if for no other reason than you know the deadline is coming. And if you know the deadline is coming you have time to take the necessary steps to achieve the deadline or communicate in advance that the deadline needs to be adjusted—in which case you won't miss the deadline.

So do yourself and your co-workers a favor and set clear deadlines, meet other people's deadlines and always always always send lots of emails and reminders and updates and check-ins at least 36 hours in advance of impending deadlines to avoid last minute surprises.

If you are the one who has work due at a deadline—plan accordingly. "Something came up" is not an acceptable excuse because something always comes up in the course of the day-to-day workflow.

If you are the one setting the deadline, invest extra time to ensure other people actually achieve your deadlines. It may strike some as patently unfair that the person setting deadlines is also responsible for ensuring their co-workers achieve the deadlines, but as the saying goes, a penny saved is a penny earned. Or, in the case of deadlines, a deadline achieved is an emotional firecracker avoided.

A few minutes spent each day reviewing your schedule and looking forward to any deadlines (given or received) can save you hours of hurt feelings, explanations and confusion later in the week. Voila, recriminations and emotions avoided—everyone wins.

Pro tip:

Most deadlines are totally arbitrary (i.e. meaningless and not tied to any real expiration), so never hesitate to suggest an alternative deadline if you anticipate difficulty in achieving the original date. For best results, recommend alternative deadlines at least 48 hours prior to the original so as to look proactive rather than unorganized and bad at your job.

Group meetings

It's hard to make the right decision. It's even harder if five human beings are staring at you.

Whenever a group of people get together there are going to be a lot of emotional dynamics at play. This person doesn't like that person, this person wants to feel smart by making someone else look dumb, that person is angling for a promotion, on and on it goes.

My advice: Skip all that and move as many of your conversations, approvals and decisions outside of group meetings and into a more controlled environment as a way to avoid the complicated, often emotional dynamics of a group setting.

Most people don't realize that they have the power to control where, when and how decisions and approvals get made. Just because your boss said they'd decide on Friday doesn't mean you have to wait until the end of the week to start communicating with the critical influencers and decision makers.

Whenever I need someone's approval (big or small) I try to get them all of the information they need as early as possible so that they have time to digest and ask questions outside the spotlight of high pressure, everyone-is-watching, we-only-have-a-few-minutes team meetings. Usually these pre-reads take the form of a simple email or discussion in our weekly 1:1 meetings.

The benefit of this approach is twofold: First, it takes the pressure off of me having to perform "in the moment" in front of a lot of people. Second, it leaves room for more organic, less pressure filled back and forth dialogue. The result of which is usually better decisions and easier approvals.

So do yourself and your boss a favor by avoiding the glare of artificially high pressure group meetings.

Midyear and end of year reviews

No one likes to feel judged, and in the workplace it's equally accurate to say that managers don't like to do the judging. Further complicating matters is the fact that most bosses suck at being bosses so neither party is set up for success when it comes to these formalized, judgmental moments on the HR calendar.

Needless to say, emotions tend to run high on both sides.

I've written extensively on the procedural do's and don'ts of promotions and end of year reviews from both the perspective of the employee and the manager in my books *How to be great at your job* and *How to be a boss*—and the one thing they both have in common is this: No one likes surprises, so it is incumbent upon everyone involved to set expectations well before the final meeting.

If you are the employee, it's best to employ a three step process: Clearly tell your boss what you want, align on what it will take to get there and then do the work. When it gets close to review time (midyear/end of year), make the extra effort to recap your performance via a crispy bullet point email and re-state your expectations at least two months prior to the deadline in order to give yourself time to resolve any lingering issues or course correct based on feedback.

If you are the boss, remember that what feels like a tough conversation now will feel like an emotional dumpster fire if you wait until review time to have it. Save yourself (and your employee) and be honest and give specific feedback along the way.

No news is not good news, so talk to each other. Treat each other as you'd want to be treated and most of the emotional strain around midyear and end of year reviews can be gracefully avoided. Win/Win.

Pro tip:
Timing is everything

Small tensions and disagreements are going to happen at work and the best thing to do is acknowledge and address them right away. If you sense that someone was disappointed by a decision or felt slighted by an interaction, reach out right away to resolve the issue.

Carrying around small grudges or indignations won't accomplish anything.

It's not a matter of who is right and who is wrong. It doesn't matter whether you or they actually made a mistake or misunderstood the issue, all that matters is that you acknowledge the interaction and resolve it simply and quickly. This effort (and timing) can help to keep small tensions small and protect your emotional well-being in the long run.

For best results, take action within 24 hours.

3. Dealin
with
disapp

ointment

3. Dealing with disappointment

There are big injustices and small inconveniences every day in every office in the world.

Whether having to deal with bad bosses, disappointing results, underperforming co-workers or just simply an unanswered email, feelings of frustration or disappointment are a fact of worklife.

The question is how you choose to emotionally process these experiences and then what you choose to do about it. Are you going to blame others or take responsibility? Are you going to inflame the conflict or de-escalate and problem solve?

Learning how to manage conflict, disappointment, frustration or feelings of being overwhelmed is a critical part of your emotional development in the workplace. In addition to recognizing and managing these feelings in yourself, it's critically important to be able to understand how being disappointed can manifest in your co-workers. This is both so you can help when appropriate but also (as importantly) protect yourself from the resulting storm of emotions.

Some people shut down, others eat their feelings and still others tend to act out with a sharp comment or a change in their tone of voice.

Your boss and co-workers don't yell at each other because they are upset about a missed deadline, they yell at each other because they are actually worried about three other deadlines hanging over their head, a dismissive interaction with a co-worker at lunch or a sick kid at home. Put simply, they are feeling overwhelmed, frustrated or anxious and their emotions are taking over.

Recognizing the signs of these emotions can save you from the temptation to escalate or personalize what might actually just be a cry for help from a co-worker or direct report who can't find (or is afraid to say) the words: "I'm overwhelmed and I could use a little help."

Wouldn't the world be a better place if we heard that phrase three times per day instead of the myriad emotional tangents that are acted out in the workplace?

Does it feel good to complain sometimes? Yes. Are there things that happen to us that aren't fair? Yes. Without doubt, there is sometimes solace in commiserating with others, but ultimately the question becomes, so what? What are you going to do about it? Blaming others for workplace problems is easy. It's also lazy and ultimately it will be a major barrier to being happy and feeling fulfilled in your work—and life.

It's easy to feel frustrated at moments when unrealistic deadlines combine to meet unforeseen one-off tasks and co-workers fail to do what they were supposed to do but it's important to keep perspective and realize that the solution usually involves a series of small actions rather than grand gestures or emotions.

- Be honest
- Ask questions
- Stop complaining
- Take responsibility

Be honest

Using honesty as a baseline approach allows you to skip over 90 percent of the noise of politicking, backstabbing, positioning and mental gymnastics otherwise required to get through just a single day at work, let alone a thirty or forty year career.

Your co-workers are smarter than you think and navigating the ups and downs, ins and outs of each other's feelings can be intimidating, exhausting and often times impossible, so it's best to keep things simple and tell the truth.

People know if something isn't going well. People know if someone is in trouble. People know if you don't like them. Co-workers know if you are hung over. Co-workers know if all you care about is yourself. Bosses know if you are disappointed or frustrated with them—so your best strategy is not to expend energy trying to convince them otherwise, but rather, go with the flow and tell the truth.

While this may seem like common sense it's surprising how often people will turn themselves into pretzels when faced with the need to have a conversation with another human being.

Telling the truth has the effect of short circuiting any potential drama lurking in work's daily to-dos and inevitable disappointments (big and small). If your co-workers know you will tell the truth, they'll trust you. If your team sees that you aren't afraid to admit when you made a mistake, they will respect you and maybe even give you the benefit of the doubt.

If you are the boss, tell the truth. Say the thing. If someone complains too much, tell them they complain too much and explain why that is undercutting their case for getting what they want. If someone is sucking at their job, acknowledge the situation and invest your energy in helping to improve their performance rather than wasting your (and their) time dancing around the elephant in the room.

Pro tip:

Another form of being honest is being willing to say what you want. Your boss isn't a mind reader, so you can't be disappointed in what you didn't get if no one knew that's what you wanted. So step up and speak your truth—you'll be surprised how much people want to help you get what you want if you can make it easy for them to understand.

Ask questions

A lot of conflict at work can trace its origins to a lack of communication—so before you jump to conclusions, start hurling accusations or trade in speculative gossip with people who have their own agendas (which are usually different from yours), it's a good idea to ask questions.

If you are disappointed in a decision, ask the person why they made it as opposed to assuming you know why and immediately dismissing their actions as wrong. Letting go of assumptions and replacing them with facts can go a long way in alleviating the emotional gymnastics of wrestling with a frustrating setback.

The formulation is simple: Asking questions is always better than making assumptions.

The less you are talking, the more you are learning, so get in the habit of shutting up from time to time and don't fall into the trap of asking leading questions. The more simple and straightforward your question—the more revealing the answer. For example, don't ask: "Did I get left out of the NYC trip because I was late to work last week?" Try instead: "Why didn't I get to travel to NYC with the rest of the team?"

A well-timed question can open doors to understanding and insight that might have otherwise never revealed themselves. It can also help to defuse a tense moment of disappointment while shifting the burden of explanation to the other person.

Stop complaining

It's easy to complain about work—that's why everyone does it.

Talking trash about a bad boss and poor performing co-workers is a right of passage. Especially early in your career it's natural to seek camaraderie and attention by belittling the people and decisions around you. In fact, it's often the people who complain the loudest that tend to be the most popular as a result of the perverse human instinct to seek comfort (or strength) through the diminishment of others.

Most people can go through their entire career and never realize they've allowed themselves to be the victim—experiencing work as one unfair decision after another. It becomes a habit, a crutch, a convenience to blame office politics for their disappointments (big and small).

But in the end, complaining is a cheap high that provides no emotional sustenance and certainly doesn't do anything to improve your circumstances and opportunities. Not to mention the emotional toll of always being the victim. The effect on your mood and your relationships (at work and at home) may be subtle, but they are certain and detrimental.

The choice is simple. Do you want to spend the next 40+ working years of your life as the victim of your surroundings or do you want to spend that time as someone who has a say in what happens to you and your career?

Complaining to your co-workers might feel good in the

moment but you should realize that they are likely to talk to other people about your complaint. Whether that talk is intentionally gossipy and hurtful, or just social chatting, it will still create a lot of noise with leadership that ultimately undermines rather than enhances your prospects.

No one likes a complainer, so if you find yourself prone to complaining about this or that—stop it. It's addition by subtraction. If you stop complaining, then you are more than halfway to having a positive attitude that puts you that much closer towards getting what you want.

Pro tip:

I have two rules when it comes to complaining. My first rule is that you aren't allowed to complain about anything unless you offer at least one viable alternative solution. My second rule is that you can complain about something once but then you need to move on. Bringing up the same complaint three times isn't going to help your cause because it will make you look selfish and distracted. By following this simple formulation you should be able to avoid the career-killing label of being a complainer.

Take responsibility

If someone doesn't reply to your email it's not because they are lazy or they don't like you—maybe it's because you didn't write a good email. If you didn't get promoted when you wanted to it's not because your boss hates you—maybe it's because you weren't willing to put in the work to avoid a surprise ending. If someone at work hates you, it's not because they "suck"—maybe it's because you haven't made a genuine effort to connect with them on a personal level.

The myriad of disappointments and frustrations you experience on a daily, sometimes hourly basis at work can look and feel a whole lot different when you stop blaming other people and instead take personal responsibility for everything that happens to you at work: the good, the bad, the frustrating, and even the unfair.

Important note: I want to pause right here to say explicitly that there is a big, important difference between frustrating and unfair vs. dangerous or illegal. If someone at work is treating another person in ways that reflect clear violations of acceptable workplace conduct, it is incumbent upon everyone involved (including bystanders) to report that behavior to HR, senior leaders or if appropriate, the police or other authorities.

This idea of self-determination is a powerful one because it means that your success in the workplace is not dependent on the kindness or caliber of people around you, but rather your own effort and willingness to work hard to make good things happen.

The implementation is simple: When something goes wrong, rather than blaming anyone else, your first instinct needs to be: What could I have done to make this situation turn out differently?

Is there ANYTHING I could have done to have improved the outcome to be more to my liking? And the thing is, the answer to these questions is always yes. There is ALWAYS something you could have done more of—or differently—to have influenced the events (and emotions) swirling around you. At the very least, go back to the first three steps in this chapter (Be Honest, Ask Questions, Stop Complaining) and go from there.

So the next time you feel disappointed by someone or something, no matter how big or small, try it out, ask yourself the simple question and see what it feels like to realize you can claim control of your own destiny. Taking radical personal responsibility is a learned behavior that becomes a habit—and from there, your experience of work will never be the same.

For some people this will be a welcome realization, for other's a disappointing reality—because to acknowledge that we have the power to change our circumstances requires us to actively choose between the lazy convenience of being a victim and the burdensome orientation towards responsibility and action.

The choice is yours.

Pro tip:
Jealousy is counterproductive

If you work in an office, it is easy to fall into the trap of comparing yourself to your co-workers as a way of validating and judging your own performance.

The trouble with this approach is that we apply these comparisons in an uneven and haphazard manner, picking and choosing the comparisons that suit a particular moment or insecurity without seeing the larger picture.

Most often, this takes the form of comparing ourselves to the worst performers to make us feel good about ourselves, and conveniently ignoring other factors that don't serve our internal narrative. There are billions of people on earth and yet we tend to judge our self-worth and professional success against a ridiculously small subset of co-workers and classmates.

Compounding this distorted perspective is our inclination to focus on what we don't have rather than being able to enjoy the moment and be grateful for all the things going well. Rarely if ever do we find ourselves able to be happy and content in our own situation.

Often times these feelings of jealousy manifest in unhealthy behaviors such as an inclination to tear other people down, talk trash on our co-workers or erode our own sense of self-worth and accomplishment. The latter self-inflicted wound being among the most unhealthy of all.

So before you expend your energy in pursuit of narrow comparisons, zoom out and seek a broader perspective. It may be helpful to remember they aren't going to list the speed of your last promotion on your tombstone.

4. How to cry at work

4. How to cry at work

The conventional wisdom says don't cry at work. That's probably the advice your dad would give you and there is a lot to be said for following this simple truth: don't cry at work and you won't need to worry about how to cry at work or when to cry at work or what it means that you cried at work. So I start by acknowledging there are a lot of advantages to completely skipping this complicated yet natural human behavior in the workplace.

Having said that, I would argue that denying yourself or those around you their right to express their feelings through the simple act of crying can be an unhealthy and unrealistic way of going about your workday.

It's important to keep in mind that emotions are a communication tool we use to express our internal feelings to the outside world. Often times emotional outbursts such as crying, yelling, sulking, raising our voice or panic attacks are an outward expression of an internal turmoil. They reflect a failure to communicate—either with ourselves (due to a lack of self awareness) or with the people around us (for fear of being judged).

The same is also true of a co-worker's daily performance. When someone is missing deadlines, showing up to work late, taking too long to get things done, this is often a manifestation of an internal struggle—maybe insecurity about asking for help, home issues they don't want to bring to work or countless other contributing factors that all come together to make us human beings.

When it comes to emotional outbursts at work, it's easier to create room for conversation and empathy when we view them as failed attempts at communication.

Crying is a useful stand-in for all manner of emotional outbursts because it is the most glaring, everyone-is-watching manifestation of a co-worker's emotional performance. It is also important to acknowledge that "crying at work" is a thing more than "yelling at work" because crying has been gendered and stigmatized by generational stereotypes that have been handed down by our parents, bosses, co-workers, and perpetuated in movies and songs.

As we dive into this chapter about how to cry at work note that many of the same rules apply across every variety of emotional outburst, whether yelling, pouting, being snippy, rude or just plain mean.

To properly examine and understand emotional outbursts in the workplace it is important we consider all aspects of the experience, including what happens before, during and after.

- Why people cry at work
- How to respond to someone crying at work
- I lost control of my emotions, now what?
- How much crying is too much crying?
- How to avoid crying at work

Why people cry at work

People have a lot of different reasons for crying at work and it's helpful to recognize and understand that crying at work is not a one-shoe-fits-all action. There are so many legitimate reasons to cry at work, it cannot be and should not be dismissed as "weak" or "women-only" or "too emotional" or unacceptable.

And what's more, even if you think you know why the person in front of you is crying, chances are that you don't know even half the rationale.

Yes, maybe the person performed poorly on a task or project and just received difficult feedback from you as their manager. But if they start crying, it would be a mistake to assume it is because of only that task or only your feedback. We, as human beings, are much more complicated than that and as such are carrying competing and overlapping emotions with us all the time. We are juggling home life with work life with personal life with family drama and our childhood traumas as well as one thousand other worries that we haven't told anyone else about or perhaps even admitted to ourselves.

Having empathy for someone who cries at work starts by acknowledging that there are many overlapping and competing reasons that someone might start to cry. This is not intended to be an exhaustive list, but rather a helpful index of some of the most common reasons that people cry at work—which often includes reasons that have nothing to do with work whatsoever.

Work related:

- Frustration that something didn't go as planned
- Scared they might get fired
- Overwhelmed with too many things to do
- Putting too much pressure on themselves to be perfect
- Disappointed that they didn't get something they wanted
- Received surprising feedback
- Someone yelled at them

Non-work related:

- Overtired—sometimes people just don't get enough sleep
- Desperate to be seen
- Don't know how to ask for help
- Learned behavior that got them what they wanted at home growing up
- Inability to express themselves with words
- Something in their personal life isn't going well

How to respond to someone crying at work

When (not if) someone starts to cry at work, don't jump to conclusions, don't assume you have the answers, and definitely don't try to "fix" the situation in that moment. Ultimately the real reason for someone breaking down and crying in front of you doesn't matter in the moment. Your only job is to make the other person feel safe and ok.

More often than not, your best reaction is no action, but just to break it down here is a six-step guide for what to do if someone at work starts crying. We will start with the assumption that it is a 1:1 meeting, and then prescribe specific additional actions required in case it is a group setting.

Step 1: Sit quietly and don't say anything

Don't try and solve it. Don't try and be encouraging, don't say it's going to be ok, don't go looking for tissues in your drawer, just sit quietly and give the person space to let it out. Don't look away, just sit there quietly, keep eye contact available to meet theirs and express a sympathetic emotion with your facial expression.

Step 2: Wait

Wait for them to indicate they want to engage. This might be when they stop crying, this might be in the midst of their sobs, but let the person crying make the first indication, whether physical or verbal, that they are open to hearing from you.

Step 3: Offer support

Keep things short and simple with an open ended question such as: "Is there anything I can do for you?" You may not get a reply right away, so be patient (and keep sitting there quietly). It's natural that you might feel uncomfortable, but find the empathy to realize this moment isn't about you—it's about the person crying in front of you and whatever it is they are going through.

Remember, the cause of their tears might have nothing to do with work so don't personalize or offer theories or solutions. Stick to the formula of a simple open question.

Step 4:
Leave the room

Once things start to even out or calm down a bit, it's a good idea to offer to leave the room to give the person a minute to collect their thoughts. It's usually best to offer a quick explanation by saying "I'm going to step outside so you can collect your thoughts for a moment. I'll come check back with you in a few minutes." It's important that you explain why you are leaving (so the person can collect their thoughts) and it's also important that you clearly communicate your continuing support (explicitly telling them you are going to come back).

Reminder: It's important that you don't rush to this step before waiting and offering support verbally first. A preemptive, too-soon departure will undermine your good intentions of creating a safe space and instead project discomfort and shame in the situation. And don't forget to pop your head back in the room with a soft knock and ask how they are doing. It's likely the person won't feel like talking at that exact moment, so keep it light and give them an easy out such as: "How are you doing? Do you want to talk or maybe catch up later?"

Step 5:
Follow up in writing

When someone cries in front of you they are trying to communicate something. They may not know what it is they are trying to say and most likely you won't know either, but regardless of whether confusion or clarity prevails, it is important that you create room for the person crying to put words to their emotions. It's too much to seek answers in the moment and confronting someone in-person later on can itself be awkward so I recommend following up with a short email before the end of the day. Keep it simple and acknowledge what happened while leaving room for the recipient to either share more feelings or close the loop by not replying so you can both move on effectively. Try something like: *Hi Katie, I just wanted to reach out and check-in. I'm here if you need anything.*

Step 6:
Don't gossip

Gossip is a cheap high. It never helps anyone and when it comes to people crying at work, there is no benefit to passing the news along to co-workers as a juicy bit of "did you know" revelry.

Remember that you very likely have no idea the real reason(s) that person might be crying so be respectful and keep it to yourself.

Pro tip:
What about crying in a group?

If someone starts crying in a group setting, it's incumbent upon the most senior person in the room to quickly intercede with a simple announcement: "Hey everyone, let's take a five minute break and come right back. See you all at 4:45." There is no need to call out why you want to take a break (i.e. "because Chris is crying") and equally important to be specific with what time you want to get re-started. This will comfort everyone to know that this is an insignificant moment rather than a major emotional incident. After the announcement it's a good idea to get up and physically escort the person crying out of the room so they don't feel alone. A good thing to say is "Let's step outside and get some fresh air."

If someone senior in the room isn't stepping up to this moment, it can create an awkward vacuum of power so use your best judgement as to whether or not it is appropriate for you to say something. But keep in mind that it is not always your job to step up in every situation.

Sometimes, the best thing to do (for you and the person crying) is to just sit quietly and let it play out. There is no black and white when it comes to managing emotions at work.

I lost control of my emotions, now what?

Whether you've cried, yelled, or panicked—it's ok. Let's repeat that: you are going to be ok.

No matter what happened, the same rules apply, so take a deep breath and then do these three things in this order:

- Follow up
- Learn from the experience
- Let it go

Follow up

It's important that you close the loop with any individuals (or groups) who may have been impacted by your emotional outburst. You need to control the narrative and quickly establish that you have bounced back and are moving forward. Any follow up needs to take place within 24 to 48 hours so as to be connected to the situation without extending it beyond its natural lifespan.

If you shared an emotional moment of tears with an individual in a 1:1 setting it is relatively easy to follow up with a one to two sentence email that provides some context for what happened and why you cried with the underlying message pointing in the direction of you feeling better and being ready to move forward.

If your emotional outburst was more negative (i.e., yelling or other aggressive behaviors) then it is incumbent upon you to find the person and apologize before the end of the day. This can include swinging by their desk and asking if they have a minute to catch up or, if they are impossible to track down before 5pm, then you must send them an email apologizing for your behavior and saying that you'd like a chance to catch up tomorrow to clear things up.

If your emotional outburst happened in front of a larger group, it can be a little bit more tricky to follow up but the same rules apply. Keep it simple, provide some context and leave everyone with a sense that you are moving forward. This can be accomplished by asking for everyone's attention at the end of a meeting through a simple joiner such as "Hey everyone, I just wanted to apologize for X."

Learn from the experience

An isolated emotional outburst in and of itself is not the end of the world. It can even be considered a natural part of caring about what you do. The important thing is that you take a moment to understand why it happened. Was it something or someone in particular? Is the reason you reacted the way you did resolved or still lingering? What did you learn about yourself that you can apply to similar situations in the future?

It isn't always natural to self-diagnose the reason that you lost control of your emotions, so I recommend you employ a quick exercise of writing a list of bullet points under the statement I cried/yelled/panicked because:. The format of open ended bullet points will allow you to explore multiple reasons without having to justify them or overly rationalize. The more bullet points you can list, the more likely you are to get at the heart of the issue and provide a genuine insight for yourself to learn from the experience.

Let it go

After it happens, everyone else will quickly move on to the next deadline, meeting or workplace drama of the day so don't linger on the experience. If you've followed the steps of circling back and evaluating what factors led to your emotional outburst you'll be well-positioned to move forward with a clear heart and mind.

We've all had the experience of feeling better or lighter after some emotional release and so you shouldn't get in the way of those positive outcomes by dwelling on self-recriminations for having cried or otherwise gotten emotional. Life goes on and you will too.

How much crying is too much crying?

Emotional outbursts impact more than the person who is doing the crying or yelling—they affect everyone around them as well. That's why it's important to acknowledge there is in fact such a thing as "being too emotional" because when a person's inability to process or communicate consistently gets in the way of other people's ability to do the work, it's going to be an issue.

When evaluating your emotional outbursts at work, think of it this way: Every employee has an allotment of tears they are allowed to cry before it becomes a performance issue. It may be obvious to say that crying or yelling a lot at work is bad, but how do you know when you've crossed the line from an ok amount of crying into the inappropriate zone?

Here is a time table to help you determine if you are crying too much at work. The same rules apply for other emotional outbursts such as yelling or even eye-rolling, which is a form of passive-aggressive communication.

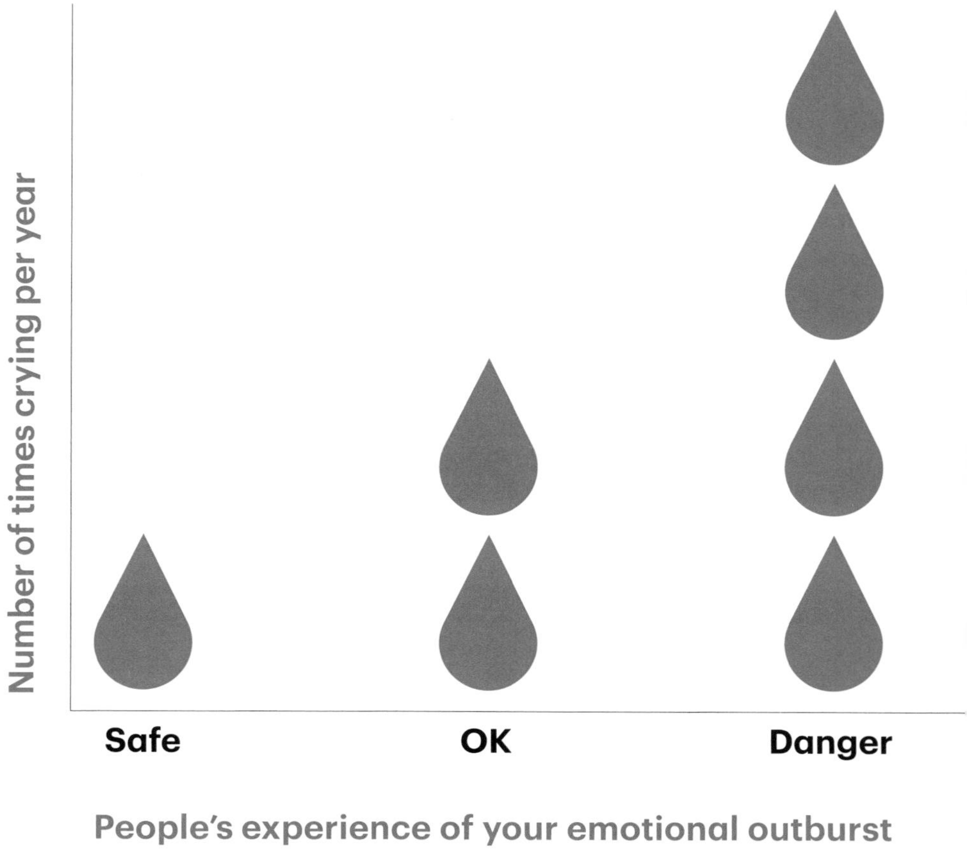

Crying Calculator

OMG **No go zone**

Here is the breakdown in more detail:

You're ok

- **Once a year (i.e. rare occasions):** Sometimes we have a bad day and that's ok. We all have our moments when life and emotions get the better of us so don't be too hard on yourself.

Danger zone

There is a problem but (likely) you don't realize it

- **"A few times per year":** If you get really emotional two or three times a year people will absolutely take your outbursts seriously and try and help you address whatever upset you. But If you are crying or yelling or acting out any more than that, such as every couple of months, it is happening regularly enough to be "a thing" and it's likely your co-workers will become dismissive—"Philip cried again"—rather than attentive. It may not be frequent enough that anyone says something to you directly but make no mistake, people are talking and it is likely to follow you around at this job and the next.

Emergency

There is a problem and everyone knows it

- **Weekly/Monthly:** If you are losing control of your emotions at work once a week or once every couple weeks there is something bigger going on and you should find someone to talk to and get help. Experiencing acute emotional moments on a weekly or even a monthly basis isn't healthy, sustainable or appropriate for work.

Check in with yourself

- **"I never cry at work"**: It's fine not to get emotional at work but take a step back and check yourself to make sure you aren't channeling your emotions through any alternative, unhealthy means of release i.e., drinking too much, losing your temper with those around you, being unable to sleep, feeling perpetual anxiety as you pull into the parking lot, etc. While these forms of emotional release and manifestation may not be as visible to your co-workers, they may be more detrimental to your health, career and well-being when compared to having an emotional outburst such as a good old-fashioned cry.

How not to cry at work

When we tend to react emotionally, it is often a reflection of an imbalance within ourselves. This can be nutritional, mental, emotional or physical.

If you are someone who finds yourself tending towards emotional outbursts across various moments in the office, here are a few quick tips that might help you reclaim ownership over your emotional performance at work.

- **Take a deep breath:** Taking slow, deep breaths is the best way to physically reclaim control of your body and if so desired, hold back an emotional outburst. There is a reason that breathing is at the center of meditation, yoga and physical performance.

- **Walk away:** Removing yourself from a moment when you feel your emotions rising can be a useful move, but it's important that you say something before you get up to leave. Otherwise you risk compounding the perception that you can't handle yourself, this moment, your emotions or this job. A simple statement (not a question) such as "I need a minute. I'll be back in five" should suffice in all settings. Use your situational awareness to determine whether this needs to be announced to the entire group in a large setting or whispered as an aside to the person next to you, effectively arming them with a controlled narrative in case someone in the room asks where you are or what you are doing. Note that I recommend being specific with your estimated return time. This specificity lends credibility that you are in control of yourself and the situation—a positive subtext.

- **Write it down:** Face to face interactions can be unpredictable and sometimes emotional. If you have a tendency to get emotional in high intensity confrontations, it may be a good idea to move the conversation to writing rather than talking. This can take the form of sending an email instead of speaking in person, but it can also be as simple as writing out your feelings as the first step in processing. Sometimes the writing is just for you, sometimes you'll share it with the other person, but regardless of how you use it, it almost always helps to get out of your head and put things on paper.

- **Say it out loud:** Holding feelings, frustrations, resentments inside can often build up pressure until it explodes—sometimes through a raised voice, sometimes through tears as a means of finally expressing the unspoken feelings. Life is too short to carry grudges or disappointments for long, so find a way to confront the issue (or person) that has wronged you so that you can move forward more freely. Having a tough conversation may not seem realistic or desirable but the alternative (not saying anything) carries its own, longer-term, emotional and psychological impact on you as well.

- **Mentors not friends:** It's important to have friends with whom to ride life's ups and downs but I generally recommend against using your friends as sounding boards for frustrations in the workplace. Absent the proper context or expertise, often times friends' advice on work-related conflicts can be counterproductive. That's why it's important that you build yourself a network of go-to mentors and peers in the workplace. Confiding in people that know you and have had numerous positive interactions with you will provide a safe landing place for your venting or confessions.

- **Get a hobby:** If you have interests and priorities outside of the workplace, you will be better prepared to absorb bad or unwelcome news or experiences with a broader context. Individual disappointments will carry less significance and therefore have less emotional impact on you.

- **Exercise:** It may sound strange to draw a direct line between exercise and emotional outbursts at work but it's true. If you exercise, you are less likely to have emotional outbursts because your mind and body have physical alternatives to release the frustrations of work. (Please excuse my pseudoscience, but this is a cliché I have found to be true).

- **Look at the big picture:** Go sit on a hill or watch the sunset. Life is much bigger than whatever it is you are dealing with at work. Having a go-to physical vantage point that provides this perspective can be a useful activity that serves to reframe the intensity of your feelings.

Bonus:
10 stories about crying at work #icried

Trading stories about other people crying at work is a workplace tradition, but I wanted to try something different. I asked people to share stories about when they cried at work as a way of de-stigmatizing and de-gendering crying, moving it from something we make fun of or gossip about into something we acknowledge, share and gain insight from. It's not about celebrating crying, it's about acknowledging it as a natural part of being human at work.

These are real stories from real people. Some wished to remain anonymous.

How about crying during a job interview?

I had been let go from one job at age 47 and I had never felt so depressed. I was desperate for work and to pay my bills. During an interview for a job that I didn't want, the managers asked me who my hero was. I thought of my teenage daughter, who is so sunny and has her whole life ahead of her. I said her name, and I burst out into uncontrollable tears. Just thinking about her optimism made me realize how low I had sunk. The managers shifted in their seats.

I finally rebounded with a joke. "Damn, I should have just said Michelle Obama." Everyone laughed uncomfortably. Needless to say, I didn't get the job.

— *Anonymous*

You're leaving me?

My first employee at my startup told me she was resigning and as she kept talking, tears started to well up in my eyes. I had worked with her for three years through thick and thin, good and bad and here she was, giving me a full three months notice. She was so graceful in that moment, I was crying at just how kind she was. We both knew she would be leaving me all alone with a growing/failing startup. I took a few deep breaths (so as not to cry too much) and told her how much I appreciated her—and that's when the tears really started coming! I was 43 at the time, and the CEO of the company.

— *Daniel*

I cry when I fire people

I took over running a small creative studio when I was 27 years old and part of my responsibilities was having to lay people off when money got tight. I was coached to be decisive and unafraid to make hard choices. I was told that "hire slow, fire fast" was a winning formula. But when you look someone in the eye and tell them this will be their last day at the company and their whole world seems to come crashing down in front of them, that false sense of BS masculine pride completely falls away. I was crushed.

In most occasions, I couldn't help but start crying right there in that moment, if not immediately afterwards. The humanity of the situation hit me like a ton of bricks. It took me months to recover. Every time. But, what I've learned is that being the "boss" means your responsibility for empathy and care for individuals in those moments is not a nice-to-have, but a duty. It was a very difficult lesson, but one I'm glad I learned.

— *Matt*

Mean girls

I felt like I was living in a bad movie. Everyone had a bad attitude, everyone was mean to each other, complained about everything and I didn't trust my boss. I felt like a shell of a person and when we had team meetings I wouldn't say a word. I'd just sit there silently and hold back everything I wanted to yell at my coworkers. I confided all of this to my mentor and much to my surprise, she must have told my boss because at the next team meeting my boss stopped the meeting and said: "Team, Alexis has the floor, let's hear what she has to say to us..." I froze. I told her I didn't have anything to add and then I quickly excused myself to run outside and cry on the phone to my mom, or boyfriend—I don't remember which.

— *Alexis*

The truth hurts?

Prior to starting my new role as the Senior Vice President at a major international retailer, I was asked to participate in a 360 feedback exercise that included anonymous, confidential feedback from the people who I worked most closely with—my managers, peers and direct reports. I knew I was a great boss, my teams loved me and my business results were amazing so I was excited to get the good feedback. Holy shit, was I way off!

I started crying about a quarter of the way through reading the results and by the end I was sitting on the floor in the corner of my office, sobbing gut-wrenching tears. I was a mess, mascara, tears, tissues everywhere.

It was at this moment that my boss knocked on my door. She had been in the office next door and heard me crying—and she knew I was reviewing my feedback results. She walked in, shared her own personal leadership journey and then gave me the best piece of advice of my career—she said it was my choice to accept the challenge or not.

She encouraged me to look at feedback as a gift and treat the challenges as opportunities.

I was 35 years old at the time but that moment is still with me and I tell that story to all my employees as a lesson in leadership and emotional fortitude. It's ok to break down but it's also important that you get up.

— Sheryl

No tears here

I've never cried at work.

— Calvin

Getting back to work

I've only cried at work one time. It was my first day back from maternity leave and I was in a closet (literally a closet) pumping breast milk. Every bone in my body told me that I needed to be home with my four month old son James but instead here I was doing extremely trivial things like resetting my logins and passwords. I cried a few tears and went back to work.

— Amy

The day Elliot Smith died

It was late afternoon on October 21, 2003, when I learned that musician Elliott Smith had committed suicide. At the time, I was working as the Director of New Media for a multinational magazine, reporting to the CEO and publisher.

Given his struggles with substances and mental illness, I wasn't shocked to hear that Elliott Smith had taken his own life, but I was suddenly and deeply saddened. When I heard the news, I remember wanting to connect with somebody who could understand the magnitude of the loss for the independent music community, so I walked outside to call a musician friend. But when I got outside, I didn't call anyone—I just broke down crying and stood there for ten minutes on the outer edge of the parking lot where no one could see me. When I was done, I wiped my eyes and walked back inside and started working.

For a long time, I wasn't even sure why I cried. I loved Elliott Smith's music, had seen him play several times and had even been introduced to him by mutual friends, but I didn't know him. In retrospect, I realized his songs were the soundtrack to a period in my life that had ended a few years prior to his death—a phase that included the end of a positive long term relationship and the death of my father—so when I heard the news, it triggered something intensely personal. It's now clear that I was crying for myself and mourning my own loss.

I still can't listen to Elliott Smith without some of those feelings coming back.

— *Brent*

I'm getting a divorce

When I told my boss I was getting a divorce, I cried. In response, she stopped everything she was doing and took me to lunch. I told her I would be going to therapy and I would need to leave early once a week. She didn't blink. She told me she would support me any way she could.

When I told the team I managed I was getting divorced, I cried again. When I told my peers and immediate co-workers, I also cried. I told everyone I was going to have good days and bad days and that I would be transparent with them if I was going through a particularly bad day (so they didn't take it personally). I was also open with them about therapy and the steps I was taking for self-care to get through this tough time. The way my boss, my team and my co-workers showed up for me in that moment was incredible. I realized that by engaging in vulnerable conversation with coworkers about myself, I gave them permission to be open about things going on in their own lives as well. Since that moment nine months ago, I have had more real, honest conversations than I experienced in the previous 15 years of my working career. The relationships that were built from this shared moment of vulnerability provided me with an unexpected support system and friendships that I will have for the rest of my life.

It doesn't always have to be about crying, but now I know that removing the stigma of mental health and self-care in the work environment is something I will prioritize for the rest of my life for myself and my teams.

— *Kelly*

Me and Lady Gaga

It was a Tuesday afternoon in December around 10am and I just started crying—big, loud, puddle drop tears.

I got up from my desk and walked into a room and shut the door. I sobbed for a good two or three minutes until someone knocked on the door because they had the room booked for a meeting. I quickly chirped "just a minute" and collected myself and walked back out to the open floor seating at my desk. I sat down, made eye contact with my boss, the founder of the company, and I immediately burst into tears again. This time even louder than the last.

I got up, pushed my way back into the room and closed the door, only to be followed by my boss stepping inside with me. I started crying. He looked at me quietly for as long as he could stand it and then said "What is it? What can I do?" and I replied "I just want to cry..."

Again, he sat as quietly and patiently as he could—probably twenty seconds that felt like twenty minutes—and then offered "I think you should go home" to which I snapped "I can't! I have so much going on today." After a brief back and forth, he convinced me that the company would survive an afternoon without me in the office and I closed my computer and walked out.

Why was I crying? I had no idea, but my gosh the tears were unstoppable. I walked home, cried some more, then decided to go see the movie *A Star is Born*. It was a Tuesday afternoon at 3pm in a nearly empty theatre and I proceeded to projectile cry through the entire movie. Even during the happy parts when Lady Gaga sings those amazing songs. It got to the point that the two or three other people in the theatre kept turning around in disbelief, concern, or frustration that there was a 40-year-old man who wouldn't stop crying.

In hindsight, I came to realize that I was crying because we had accomplished our goals for the year but I felt empty inside. We had announced earlier in the week that everyone would receive a bonus and rather than being a cause for celebration and congratulations, it was met with a whimper. I had never worked harder to make something happen in my entire work life and at the moment of declared victory there was deafening silence.

My tears were a release of stress as well as a cry of injustice. Was no one going to recognize the efforts I'd made? It was a useful reminder to me that work is work and wrapping too much of yourself into the workplace is not a healthy behavior. I'd lost balance and lost perspective.

Six weeks later I told my boss I wanted to quit. I realized that I had run out of momentum and couldn't keep giving everything I had if it wasn't going to make me feel fulfilled.

— *Justin*

5. Manag
stress

ing

5. Managing stress

While the high drama of emotional outbursts such as crying or yelling may get everyone's attention, the mental and emotional strain of a persistent, low level feeling of stress is cumulative and can be even more detrimental to your health and ability to function effectively in the workplace.

Anxiety is your body's natural response to stress. It's usually a feeling of apprehension about what's to come—and at work there is always something to come: a deadline, a presentation, a meeting, another meeting and then more meetings, all of which adds up to feeling stressed about when you are going to have time to get all your work done.

Being stressed at work takes many forms, from the generic low level "There is a lot going on" and "I'm super busy" to the more intense "I'm feeling stressed" or the fatalistic "I'm overwhelmed and I can't do this."

Stress has a way of blinding people to the reality of any given situation. A small thing can feel like a big thing when you're anxious, and big things turn into impossible things when the stress is intense enough. Suffice to say that feeling stressed is more than unpleasant. It's counterproductive.

One side effect of feeling stressed at work is that you start to think too much. You start feeling all the feelings and thinking all the things and before you know it you're paralyzed with anxiety, unsure where to start, stuck in your own head. When you find yourself in these moments it's best to stop thinking and start doing.

Here is a simple three-step process for managing anxiety and finding your way beyond stress at work:

- Make a list
- Ask for help
- Do the work

Make a list

The first step to resolving stress is to get whatever is bothering you out of your head and onto a piece of paper. This has the immediate effect of turning "feelings" into tasks. It's important not to overthink it, just start writing.

I like to recommend bullet point lists as an effective, open ended way to start because their format supports incomplete thoughts while separating one idea from another visually. Look at your calendar and go meeting by meeting or project by project to help spark your memory of all the little things that you need to get done or identify the meetings that cause anxiety.

When putting together your list be sure to break "big" issues into smaller parts.

It isn't useful to say "I'm never going to get everything done." Instead be as specific as possible by listing every single thing that needs to happen: "I need to reply to Adam's email. I need to remind Casey about that deadline. I need to spend 3 hours working on this presentation. I need to reschedule my dentist appointment. I need to send an agenda for my 1:1 with Justin tomorrow. I need to follow up with Daniel. I need to spend an hour teaching Cat how to fill out her budget reports. I need to..."

By breaking down your anxieties (and maybe insecurities?) into a bullet point list of tasks, you've given yourself the best chance possible to stop stressing and start improving.

Pro tip:

Once you have your bullet point list it's a good idea to prioritize from easiest to most difficult. I recommend this method of organization because the process of getting out from under your feelings of doubt and anxiety is a gradual climb. More often than not there are small things we can cross off the list right away, providing a confidence boost and sense of accomplishment right from the start, and helping to build momentum on getting things done.

Ask for help

Now that you have your list, you need to start doing the work, and often your first, best move should be to ask for help. Although it may be intimidating in the moment, asking for help is your best chance at liberating yourself from the emotional burden and distraction of feeling "under pressure" or constantly behind.

A request for help can take a lot of different forms. Maybe ask to move a deadline—sometimes even a few hours can make a difference. Maybe ask for help prioritizing three competing priorities—often times your boss or co-worker doesn't realize that they've prioritized everything so bringing it to light usually helps everyone involved. It might even eliminate to-dos that are no longer relevant.

A simple request for help might sound something like this: "I've noticed that I really don't feel as confident as I want in this meeting. It seems like you're really good at knowing where to look in the report for answers. Can you walk me through your process, really slowly, and explain how you read this report?"

There are three key points to include in any request for help. The first is to humble yourself in order to create a safe space. By showing your vulnerability ("I don't feel as confident as I want"), you invite the other person into your world in an authentic way. The second step is to recognize other people's skills with some subtle flattery ("it seems like you're really good at..."). Then finally, ask for help by being very very specific in what you want to get from the experience ("explain how you read this report"). The more specific your request, the more likely you are to gain insight rather than generic platitudes.

Asking for help isn't always easy, especially when it is shrouded in the emotional fog of self-consciousness or insecurity, but keep in mind that people like to help people, so don't suffer in silence or resign yourself to late days and unending stress. Instead, send a quick email asking for help or tap someone on the shoulder and ask "Do you have five minutes?" You can also use your weekly 1:1 meeting with your boss to admit that you're struggling with topic X and you'd like their advice on how to get better. Sometimes the right thing is the obvious thing.

Pro tip:

Showing self awareness is always a good idea.

Do the work

At some point, there's nothing left to do but put your head down and get to work. But while this might be an obvious solution to a specific impending deadline, it also provides a deeper, more meaningful way to de-stress your work life. Namely: practice.

Nobody was born with the ability to write good emails and no one was put on this earth to fill out Google Sheets. More often than not, the only difference between a top performer (or efficient worker) and a middling employee is the amount of practice and/or training they have had doing a particular task.

I often tell new hires that you need to go through something three times before you can have any chance at being good at it—a new meeting, a new process, a new spreadsheet. The first time you go through something you have no idea what you're doing. The second time is the most dangerous because you think you know what you're doing (but actually you don't) and it isn't until the third time that you can achieve some semblance of adequacy.

Practice is the surest way to bridge the gap between stress-inducing slow performance and confidence boosting, efficient task to-doing.

So if you want to solve the underlying issues of stress, it's going to take work and a commitment to practice outside of the intense pressure of an impending deadline. Getting better at your job takes time. It's a series of small improvements which eventually add up to noticeable changes.

It's a journey, not a destination so trust in the fact that the more time and energy you put into mastering (i.e. practicing) a certain skill, the less time you will spend worrying about that part of your job.

Pro tip:

Saying that you don't have time to practice is a lame excuse. There is always more time (get into work early, take a shorter lunch, stay late one or two days a week for two or three weeks). Voila, you're good at your job, which means less stress. Nice work.

6. Health vs. hangry

6. Healthy vs. hangry

Being good at your job includes being good at taking care of yourself—mentally, physically and emotionally. While most of this book covers the emotional aspects of work, it's important that we highlight some of the most common mistakes people tend to make as it relates to staying physically healthy and mentally balanced.

- Hangry
- Tired
- Unbalanced

Hangry

Hungry + angry = hangry.

Being hangry is a thing. We laugh at those Snickers commercials because they are true.

Normal, easy going people can turn into grouchy curmudgeons if they haven't had enough to eat or drink. When it comes to work, the biggest issue is you often don't realize the effect being hangry has on your attitude, performance and reputation.

When you don't eat right your body doesn't feel right, your mind doesn't work right and your emotions don't act right. So pay attention to how you feed the machine because taking care of your body is as important to being effective at your job as sending good emails.

Everyone is different so I don't need to prescribe what to eat or when to eat it. Instead, I'll simply offer my hard earned wisdom that eating mashed potatoes at lunch during a workday will more often than not lead to you falling asleep later in the day (usually during a boring meeting). This happened to me twice during my first year out of college while working at Gap headquarters.

Suffice to say it didn't impress my co-workers.

Getting dehydrated is a real thing too and breathing unnatural air all day will dry you out so figure out how to drink at least two to three glasses of water per day while you're in the office. Oh—and don't drink too much coffee. When people drink too much coffee they get antsy, and when they get antsy, they get emotional and no one likes a coffee-fueled hangry co-worker.

Tired

When people get tired, they tend to get emotional.

This might be as simple as a sleepless night with the kids or a long night at the bars, but whatever the reason, it's important to acknowledge the impact it has on your ability to show up emotionally for yourself and the people around you.

A few easy workarounds when you find yourself tired at work can be chugging a Redbull (just kidding, you don't have to chug it), taking a walk around the block to get some fresh air and exercise or admitting that you don't have it in you today and informing co-workers that you are going to leave early.

On a personal level, as I've gotten older, I've realized just how much a lack of sleep can impact my emotional performance at work. As a result I've had to admit to myself that drinking during the work week just isn't worth it anymore. Feeling lethargic and ever-so-slightly disconnected from what's happening around me is too high of a price to pay when I have a team of people looking up to me and watching my every move—good and bad, subtle and overt.

Pro tip:

Another common cause of tiredness is the fact that people suck at taking vacations.

Vacations (big and small) are not only an important part of staying healthy, they're also a great way to check your ego, and remind you that no matter how important you think you are, the work still manages to get done if you aren't in the office.

Unbalanced

Human beings are complicated creatures and we require a multitude of inputs and outputs to be at our best in life and at work.

By getting too wrapped up in work, it's easy to lose the ability to separate yourself from your work and this is an unhealthy territory to exist in from day-to-day. It means every interaction, every little piece of feedback will feel like a judgement on you personally rather than a normal project-related correction or improvement.

The result is that small things feel like big things because you've lost perspective, which can make you overreact to a misspelled word, a mediocre presentation or a messy workspace.

Being on edge or overly sensitive isn't a fun experience for anyone involved, so do yourself and your co-workers a favor and find something you like to do outside work.

It doesn't matter what it is. It could be beekeeping, it could be coaching your kid's soccer team, it could be learning to throw pottery. The point is that you have something to get you out of your head and help you let go of work for a few hours. If the obvious choice of going to the gym isn't for you, I'd recommend you stimulate your "beginner's mind" and take a class.

Learning to do something new will help you access empathy and give immediate perspective to everything you still have to learn in the world.

Another way to find (and keep) balance is to take a break every now and then.

While vacations are the obvious available structure for a break from work, I would encourage you to be creative in finding small breaks throughout your day and work week. This can be as simple as a walk around the block when you have an extra five minutes or sitting outside to eat your lunch rather than rushing back to your desk. Step outside to make/take a phone call. These small moments/breaks can be just enough to keep your mind and energy fresh and balanced during a long work week.

I promise that an extra five minutes spent outside during your workday will more than pay off in your daily emotional performance and operational productivity.

Many companies now offer personal days as a subsidy of their paid time-off package. While many people simply lump these in with the rest of their PTO allotment, I would encourage you to distinguish these gifts from your sick days or vacation days. Taking a day off work midweek can be totally refreshing for the very fact that it feels "weird" to not be at work on a Wednesday.

It also can help relieve stress by giving you a chance to take care of a bunch of stuff that's been hanging over your head for months that you never have time to get to.

Pro tip:

Breathe. You can call it meditation or not, that's up to you, but the simple act of sitting still, closing your eyes and focusing on your breathing—even for just two minutes—can have a revelatory effect on your mental and emotional state. If you drive to work, sit in your car for thirty seconds with your eyes closed before you open the door to head into the office. If you take the bus or train, close your eyes for thirty seconds between stops. Try it; you can thank me later.

7. Good vibes

Good vibes

When it comes to emotional performance in the workplace we can tend to focus on the weightier issues of crying, giving feedback or dealing with bad bosses and unrealistic deadlines. But finding ways to lift people's spirits and break the monotony of the staid, safe, artificially quiet office environment can be equally important to finding and maintaining our emotional equilibrium at work.

In this chapter we will focus on easy ways to bring positive energy into our work lives. After all, let's not forget that we are spending more time during the week with our co-workers, than we do with our friends and family—so why not try and enjoy it.

- Nine ways to connect with your co-workers
- Clapping is a secret weapon

Nine ways to connect with your co-workers

I take for granted a general principle that people want to help people—we are all generally nice that way. But it's important to understand that people want to help people they like even more.

As I talk about in my book *How to be a boss*, it's easy for people in the workplace to lose their humanity and start treating each other like task rabbits, stuck in an endless loop of meetings, reports and emails. It's your job to make sure this doesn't happen. It's your responsibility to invest a little extra effort in connecting with the people around you on a regular basis in order to keep up relationships or form new ones.

Even the smallest acts of gratitude or acknowledgement can go a long way to creating the type of work environment where everyone can be their best self, ready to support and encourage (and forgive) the people they spend eight to ten hours a day with.

Here is a list of nine winning behaviors that should enhance your ability to work well with other human beings across the impossibly wide spectrum of workplace interactions. If they seem obvious or easy—that's the point. Being a good person doesn't take much, so stop worrying about this and that and just follow the golden rule: Do unto others as you'd have them do unto you.

1 Greet people in the morning

It may sound silly, but saying good morning when people come into the office is a leading indicator of a positive attitude. Pay attention to your tone of voice to make sure you aren't just going through the motions. People can tell the difference between genuine warmth and perfunctory platitudes. Don't forget your co-workers are human beings and they yearn to be seen, so even a simple head nod can go a long way to setting the right tone with the people around you.

2 Show enthusiasm

Let go of your teenage angst and any misbegotten notions that it's cool to not care. Showing a little bit of enthusiasm in a team meeting can go a long way toward cultivating a reputation for positivity and a good attitude. When your boss announces good news, show some emotion. When someone tells the group that you need to do a boring task, show some enthusiasm to get it done. These little moments have a tendency to add up and if you are consistently showing enthusiasm in a genuine manner, people will take notice.

3 Nod your head

Literally nod your head when you are listening to someone speak in a meeting. This can be as simple as a subtle smile, a small head nod or an enthusiastic Woop! —all of which have the benefit of providing encouragement to the speaker while also building your reputation as an engaged, enthusiastic co-worker.

4 Offer to help

Get off your butt and offer to help your co-worker carry the boxes down the hall. Offer to bring lunch back when you see someone is busy and might miss their lunch break. Offer to clean up a mess when you know someone is under deadline and might need a few extra minutes or a helping hand. Offering to help is a great way to build goodwill with your co-workers and while there may not be an immediate payback, rest assured it all comes around.

Pro tip:

Volunteer to do the one job no one else wants to do, whether collating everyone's submissions into one file, volunteering to coordinate the tech before group meetings or something as unexpected as taking out the trash. While some co-workers will think you are a sucker for doing the dirty deed, the people in charge will notice you stepping up and will appreciate your willingness to do whatever it takes to get the job done as a team player.

5 Sit next to someone new

It's easy to sit in the same seat next to your friends in every meeting but if you make the extra effort to sit in different places next to different people, you are much more likely to build connections throughout your team, which often leads to faster reply times when you send emails, quicker approvals when you have requests, and more benefit of the doubt when things go wrong.

6 One compliment per day

Rather than falling back on generalities about "being nice" or "having a good attitude" give yourself a specific, measurable goal to prove your performance. Try giving one compliment per day or set a calendar reminder for Friday afternoon that reminds you to send one nice email to a coworker before leaving for the weekend. It can be as simple as "Nice work on the presentation this week. Have a great weekend" or "Just wanted to say thanks for helping me get everyone motivated for the team lunch this week. It really made a difference for me. Thank you."

7 Celebrate

People don't celebrate enough at work. We have a tendency to run from one task to another under a constant sense that there isn't enough time to get everything done so there definitely isn't enough time—or justification—to celebrate.

But when we miss chances to celebrate, we miss a chance to build self confidence, recharge our positive emotional balance and renew motivation for the next task. We miss out on the healthy emotional release of endorphins and the related benefits of camaraderie, belonging and a sense of accomplishment.

Celebrating can be as simple as a quick round of applause, an encouraging slap on the back, a quick "nice work" or a cheesy (but fun) "raising of the roof"—in all cases it's the thought that counts.

8 Buy coffee

Spending time with and getting to know your co-workers outside of high pressure deadline moments goes a long way towards building a physical and emotional foundation upon which all other interactions exist.

If you've bought me a coffee within the last 30 days, am I more or less likely to complain about your performance? Am I more or less likely to talk shit about you with other people at work? Am I more or less likely to give you the benefit of the doubt when your tone of voice is a little more aggressive than usual? You already know the answer.

Let's do the math. If you were to make a point of buying coffee for two people every week for 50 weeks of the year, that means 100 coffees (x $4) which would cost you $400/ year of investment in your own prospects. Put another way, if I told you that you could pay $400 to have everyone at work like you, have people give you the benefit of the doubt and likely get promoted faster, would you pay that toll? Yes yes yes.

9 Say "thank you"

Too often, people feel so busy or distracted that they skip the thank you and proceed directly to the "get back to work" phase of office life, but it doesn't have to be that complicated. When it comes to saying thank you at work, the prescription is easy: If you feel it, say it. Don't overthink it, just say thank you.

The quicker you say thank you, the less explanation is needed. Someone hands you a printed report, say thank you. Someone sends you an email with information you've been waiting for, click reply and type 'Thanks.' Don't talk yourself out of sending an email thank you in the name of efficiency—or concern for filling up their inbox. I don't know of anyone in the history of the working world who has complained about receiving too many compliments. Even one word— thanks —has the power to change someone's day or motivate renewed effort on a project.

Pro tip:

If you want to be an A+ thank you giver, include a detail such as "Thanks for sending through early" or "Thanks for sending in an easy format—it really saves me time." By applying specific details to your thanks, you reinforce the behaviors you'd like to encourage, thus multiplying the power of the thank you beyond it's baseline expression of gratitude. Advantage: you.

Clapping is a secret weapon

Clapping is one of the only acceptable ways to disrupt the monotony of artificial silence that persists across offices, conference rooms and open floor plans around the world.

In scientific studies, clapping has been likened to an infectious disease, spreading amongst the crowd in the same manner, time and intensity as is recognized with infection. This is called a sigmoidal curve for those that are scientifically inclined. In a word, clapping is contagious.

But clapping is useful for more than moments of generic celebration. It's also a useful tool for reinforcing good behavior and bringing a group together around a synchronized physical activity that reminds us all that we are part of something bigger than ourselves. So clap on...

- **Teaching tool:** The power of clapping as a teaching strategy is grossly underappreciated. If you are happy with what someone has done, if you want to encourage that behavior, effort, accomplishment to be repeated, the easiest thing to do is to clap in recognition of said behavior. When other people see that you liked something, we as humans naturally want to be liked, so we in turn are more likely to mimic the awarded behavior ourselves.

  Voila, I've communicated to an entire group what my preferred behavior is without having to say a single word.

- **Team bonding:** It takes a lot of effort, planning, tools, systems, training, encouragement and sometimes intimidation to get a group of people to all do something together at the same time with the same shared goal. Clapping isn't one of those things. Clapping is easy. So the next time you take the brave step of starting a clap, realize you aren't just acknowledging effort, you are creating a moment to bond with your co-workers physically and emotionally.

- **Reputation building:** Clapping can have a ripple effect throughout the office. When sitting at your desk and hearing clapping come from a conference room or another area of the floor, people stop what they are doing and look up.

  If the first reaction is confusion or frustration, the second emotion is intrigue—what are they clapping about? It's at this moment that your clapping has become a signal to the rest of the office that good things are happening within your group, team or project. It's more than likely that later in the day, coworkers will get to talking and ask: "Why was everyone clapping earlier today?" Voila, people are talking about you and your team in a positive light and everyone likes to be on a winning team.

Pro tip:

Clapping has been shown to improve blood circulation, skill enhancement in children and with 28 pressure points in our hands the benefits are felt throughout the body. Studies have shown that clapping can even be employed as a means of therapy to combat arthritis, gout, asthma and organ health. So if you're happy and you know it, clap your hands.

Afterwor

Afterword

Attitude is everything. It's a cliche because it's true.

If you have a good attitude everything is easier (and more enjoyable). Working with other human beings is easier, being good at your job is easier and even sucking at your job is less painful because people give you the benefit of the doubt when you screw up—and what's more, they are more likely to try and help you fix the problem rather than walk away and complain about you.

I read a quote by Charles Swindoll that goes something like *life is 10% what happens to you and 90% how you react to it*—and while I may not agree with the percentage breakouts I certainly agree with the sentiment. You can't always control what happens to you—or around you in the workplace—but you can always control your attitude. And your attitude will inform your behavior and thus your emotional performance at work.

Have you ever stopped to think about whether you have a positive or negative attitude? Have you ever stopped to consider what kind of energy you are bringing to the office? Positive or negative? (Hint: there is no in-between). It's easy to tell the difference in other people, but what about in yourself?

So before you allow yourself to get bogged down in the countless emotions of the workplace, before you start to wonder whether you are "doing it right" and even before you set about learning new skills and perfecting the operational side of work, do the easy thing and bring a positive attitude and energy to every interaction.

And even if that feels impossible, understand that sometimes managing conflict is as simple as avoiding the conflict to begin with. If you stop the perpetual cycle of complaining, if you stop looking for fault and instead focus on intention, the workplace becomes a much kinder, productive space to live in.

Nobody is perfect, so it's a good idea to accept that you are going to have good moments and bad moments at work. Sometimes you'll get yelled at and sometimes you'll be the one frustrated and raising your voice. More often than not, you will not say the exact right thing at the exact right moment with the exact right tone—and that's ok.

I've spent the last five years preaching the gospel of efficiency through over-communication. My books *How to write an email*, *How to be a boss*, and *How to be great at your job* codify a simplified system of communication that can allow anyone to find sustainable success in their day-to-day work, but the topics in this book are the ones that can unlock the joy and satisfaction of working with other human beings.

When you think about emotions at work you can't just consider how you feel, but rather you must take into account the entire ecosystem of the workplace. How do other people's emotions impact you and from there, what resulting effect do you have on the people around you (peers, bosses and direct reports)? Navigating the emotional waves of the workplace isn't easy—but it also doesn't have to be hard.

There will always be new situations beyond your control or experiences which leave you grasping for what to do—and in moments such as these, trust that if you can stay attuned to your own emotions, you're more than halfway to happiness at work.

Thank you

Special thanks to Adam Katz for encouraging me to tackle this important topic as part of my survival guide series. Shout out to my co-workers at Gap and Old Navy for helping me get my start and making room for me to grow up—and screw up. Thanks to Levi's for believing in me and giving me a chance to live in Tokyo. Thanks to my UNIQLO teams in Paris, London, New York City and Tokyo for allowing me to be my best (work) self—at least most of the time. And thank you to my colleagues at Imprint Projects who were gracious in giving me room to unwind my physical, mental and emotional commitment to the work-a-day world, I appreciate your understanding and encouragement along the way. Much love to Mauri, Lucas, John, Chris, Justin, Nina, David, Lucy, Rainer, Alexis, Berndt, Q, Nicole, Casey, Sheryl, Mami, Michi, Shindo, Whitney, JC, Michele, Kazumi, Jenn, Jonathan, Ian, Josh, Daniel, Keith, Chad, Mom and Dad and everyone else who has made me laugh and cry at work.

With apologies...

I don't have enough bullet points to list every person I've wronged at work, but there's a few that deserve airing:

Apologies to Brian for trying to turn you into a mini me. Apologies to Scott for running you out of town. Apologies to Nick for talking over you during the Netflix meeting.

Apologies to Mr Yanai for breaking your trust. Apologies to Liz for acting out. Apologies to Christine for not saying good morning. Apologies to Matt for losing my patience. Apologies to LeAnn for trying to go over your head. Apologies to Robin for falling asleep. Apologies to Marilyn for writing a mean email. Apologies to Ash for not listening more closely. And to everyone else I've wronged along the way: I'm sorry—please forgive me. Writing these books has been a form of catharsis for me, affording me an opportunity to make amends by giving back and allowing me to get my things in order as I let go of the working world and start anew.

Onwards.

About the author

Justin Kerr is the author of the rogue corporate playbooks *How to write an email*, *How to be a boss* and *How to be great at your job*. Justin is also the mouthpiece of MR CORPO podcast. A self-described efficiency monster, Justin has been the youngest senior executive at some of the world's biggest apparel companies (Old Navy, Levi's, UNIQLO) running billion dollar businesses while finding time to write 15 books, tour the country with his rock band and keep 100,000 bees on his roof. He currently lives in Palm Springs, California.

Best to follow his adventures on Instagram @mrcorpo or www.mrcorpo.com. You can also reach him by email at justin@mrcorpo.com.

About the survival guide book series

Part workplace survivalist, part corporate myth-buster, Justin has set out to demystify the inner workings of office culture and empower people to make the most of their time at work. Justin has been touring the country since 2015 spreading his gospel of efficiency through overcommunication via workshops, book tours, lectures and executive coaching at companies big and small.

Justin's simple, straightforward books have become a go-to manual for tens of thousands of people around the world, being passed down from one coworker to another as a shortcut for teaching people how to be good at their job. These books fill the void between the boss' good intentions and their bad follow through—since everyone is too busy to explain the basics of what to do, what to say and what never ever to try at work no matter what.

How to write an email

This book shows you the basic behaviors that will set you apart from your peers and help you get credit for all the work you do. Whether you work at a Fortune 500 company or the latest tech start-up, the simple, actionable steps highlighted in this book will change the way you communicate forever. (My wife made me stop short of a money-back-guarantee.)

How to write an email is aimed at new employees but it's useful for anyone who wants to be great at what they do. Chapters include: The basics of being good at your job, How to give a presentation, How to write an email, How to get promoted.

How to be a boss

Being a boss is about more than bossing people around. It's hard work. And if you want to be good at it you have to get two things right: people and process. Chapters include: 9 Ways to make your team hate you, 10 ways to make your team love you, How to lead your team, How to motivate your team, How to give feedback, How to get people promoted, How to interview someone, How to fire someone, plus much more...

How to cry at work

The third installment in the survival guide series investigates how we navigate the emotions of working with other human beings as well as the surprising number of emotions involved with filling out spreadsheets, sending emails, giving presentations and missing deadlines. Chapters include: How to cry at work, Managing stress, Situational awareness, Healthy vs. hangry and more on emotional performance at work.

How to quit your job

This book will help you figure out whether or not you should quit your job. It will also instruct you on the best way to break the news, interview for new jobs and negotiate your new salary and benefits. Chapters include: Don't quit your job, Preparing to quit your job, Starting your new job and How to ask for a raise.

About MR CORPO podcast

Self-described efficiency monster Justin Kerr brings you myth busters and survival strategies from the corporate world. The MR CORPO podcast features interviews with a rotating crew of insiders, outsiders and recovering corpos plus workplace advice from Justin's rogue corporate playbooks *How to write an email, How to be a boss* and *How to be great at your job.* You can subscribe at Apple Podcasts, Spotify or anywhere fine podcasts are found.

With more than 40 episodes, topics include:

- How to give feedback
- How to be a dad (and be good at your job)
- How to set yearly goals
- Don't sit in an office
- Three things you should do everyday
- How to get sh*t done (in a big company)
- Leave the party early
- Humans vs. employees
- How to impress your new boss
- How to get your dream job
- How to network
- Bored at work
- How to set goals
- How to interview
- How to ask for help
- How to ask for a raise
- How to take vacation
- How to get promoted

#icried
mrcorpo.com
@mrcorpo
justin@mrcorpo.com

How to cry at work
A survival guide to corporate America
Justin Kerr

ECP/009

Art Direction/Design: Brian Scott/Boon
boon.design

Editing: Deanne Katz

Typography: Graphik, Tiempos

Printed by Shapco Printing, Inc.
Made in USA

First Edition: 2000

ISBN: 978-1-5323-5072-6

ExtraCurricular Press
extracurricularpress.com

This and other ExtraCurricular Press
printed matter can be ordered direct
from the publisher:
extracurricularpress.com